Yellowstone's Wild Wonders:
A Kid's Rhyming Guide

Illustrated and Written by Adam M. Wallace

To My Brave Sons Axel And Antonio,

And The Amazing Staff of the Johns Hopkins Hospital,

Your First Few Weeks Were More Of An Adventure Than

A Trip to Yellowstone.

I Cannot Wait To Go Explore With You. I Love You Both.

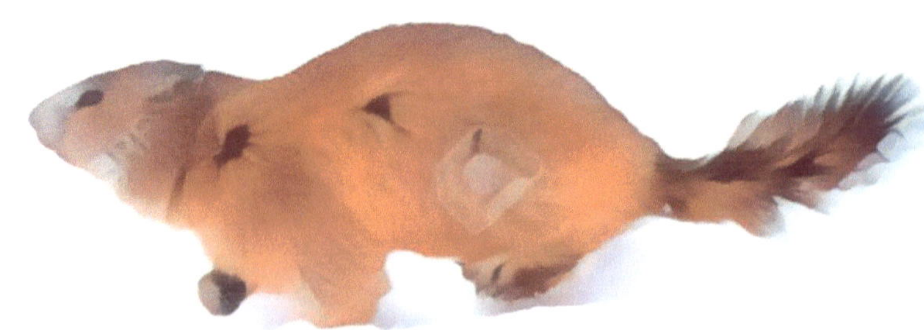

Whether there's rain, snow, or sun,
Visiting Yellowstone is always great fun.

There are many animals that roam,
And they all call Yellowstone their home.

Remember here all the creatures are wild,
Do not get too close and hold onto your child.

Buffalos stroll through fields as they munch,
Tall green grass is their favorite lunch.

In winter when the snow is deep,
All the bears take a big sleep.

Come springtime grizzlies search for food,
When they find some grub, they are in a good mood.

Always watch out for mama bear,
If you get near her cubs, she might do more than glare.

Black bears can climb
high in the trees,

Sometimes they steal
honey from the bees.

Eagles perch in the pines and fly,
They dip and dive in the light blue sky.

Beavers like to live in creeks,
And use trees to build dams without any leaks.

Big horn sheep have skulls with two layers,
To protect them when they crash like football players.

Elk like to live in a great big herd,
For miles and miles, their bugles can be heard.

The tallest animal in the park is the mighty moose,
Sometimes you can see them walking near the spruce.

Canada lynx have extra wide paws,
They work like snowshoes with long sharp claws.

Mountain Lions are hard to see,
I can't tell, is one watching me?

The Park has several wolf packs,
Look close, you might see a pup or their tracks.

Don't blink too quick,
Red fox live in dens and are really slick.

Osprey live high on the Grand Canyon rim,
While in the Yellowstone River below fish swim.

Bears use their big strong snout,
To go fishing for some trout.

Seeing animals is always fun,
But your Yellowstone adventure has just begun.

Yellowstone is full of geothermal features,
The water is home to millions of tiny creatures.

Heat and pressure make the geysers spray,
To stay safe, always keep away.

Watching the eruption of Old Faithful,
Will leave you feeling awfully grateful.

Make sure to visit Mammoth Hot Springs,
It is special and one of the park's smelliest things.

At the Norris Geyser Basin there aren't many trees,
The scalding water and acid stops all that it sees.

Boiling water bubbles from the ground,
Leaving thermal pools all around.

In the cooler parts of hot springs,
Little bacteria make colorful rings.

You can see where the water is really hot,
It is the center dark blue spot.

Heated water from the Fire Hole River,
Is nice and warm, in it you will never shiver.

Hayden Valley is a vast, open grassland,
With herds of buffalo that are most grand.

A drive through Lamar Valley,
Is a trip up wildlife alley.

As the road winds,
You will see animals of all kinds.

In the winter, the snow here can get taller than a house,
Don't leave food out or you will see more than a mouse.

Yellowstone was the world's first National Park,
It is up to you to leave no trace and make no mark.

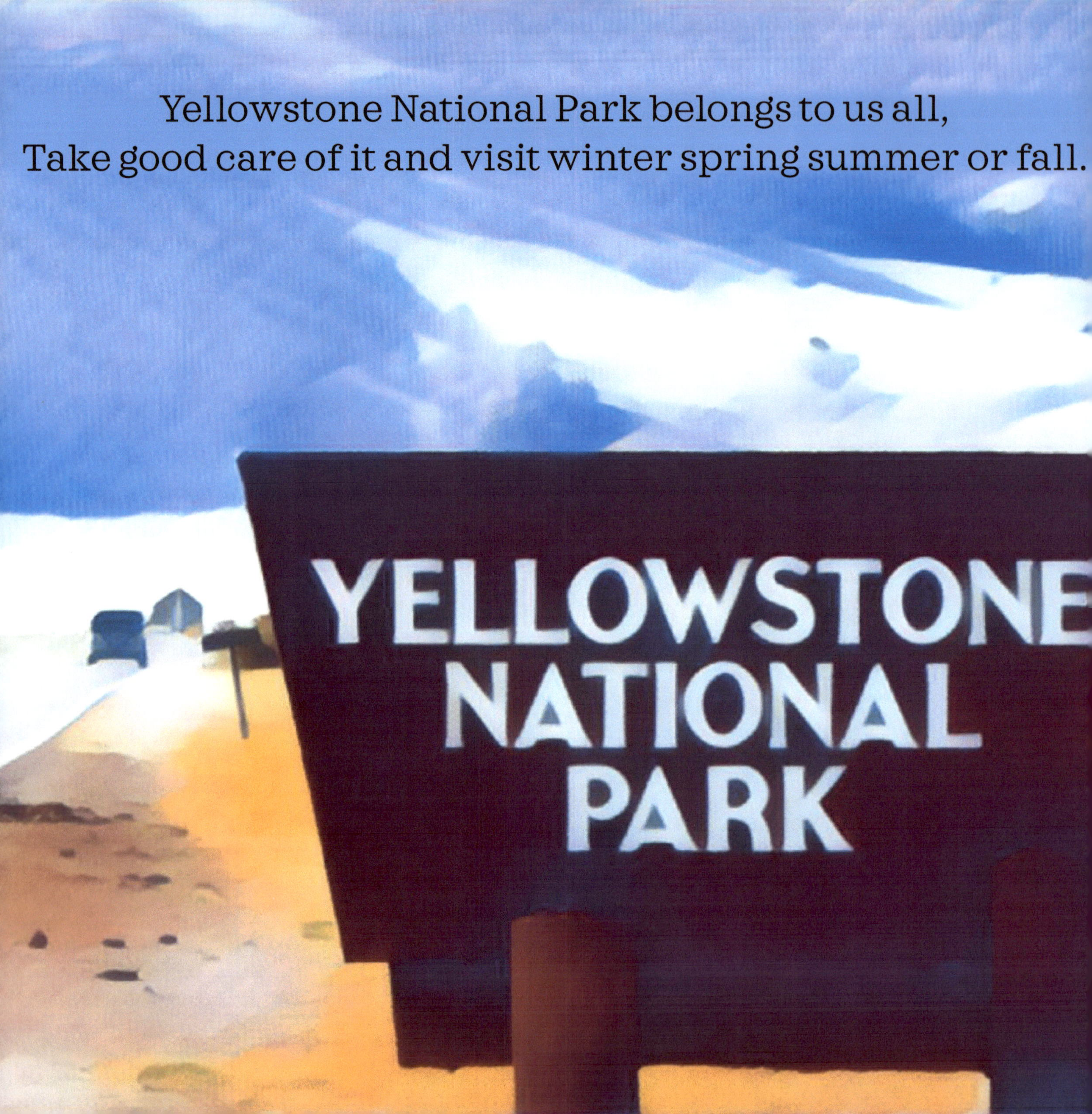

Yellowstone National Park belongs to us all,
Take good care of it and visit winter spring summer or fall.